My Brother, My Sister

Loretta Burns & Bill F. Ndi

Langaa Research & Publishing CIG
Mankon, Bamenda

Publisher:

Langaa RPCIG
Langaa Research & Publishing Common Initiative Group
P.O. Box 902 Mankon
Bamenda
North West Region
Cameroon
Langaagrp@gmail.com
www.langaa-rpcig.net

Distributed in and outside N. America by African Books Collective
orders@africanbookscollective.com
www.africanbookcollective.com

ISBN: 9956-727-26-1

About Loretta Burns

Loretta Burns is professor of English and department head at Tuskegee University. An Alabama native, she received her bachelor's degree from Tuskegee, her M.A. from Ohio State University, and her Ph.D. from the University of Michigan. She has also studied at Columbia University and the Sorbonne and conducted research at Harvard and Yale Universities. She has held faculty positions at Fisk University, the University of Florida, and Washington University in St. Louis.

About Bill F. Ndi

Dr. Bill F. NDI, poet, playwright, storyteller, critic, translator & academic hails from Bamunka-Ndop, the North West Region of Cameroon. He was educated in Cameroon, Nigeria and France where he obtained his doctorate degree in Languages, Literatures and Contemporary Civilizations. He has held teaching positions at the Paris School of Languages, the University of the Sunshine Coast at Sippy Downs, the University of Queensland, Brisbane, St Lucia and Deakin University, Melbourne, Australia. He teaches at Tuskegee University, Alabama, USA.

Table of Contents

La Belle Dame sans Choix
July South
February Spring
Within the Wheel
The Man We Killed
Worm Hole
The Old Scholar
The Homecoming
After New Orleans
For William
The Baptizing
Ax Man
Night Song
Rock Water
Peaches and Honey
Nashville
Meeting
A Little Blues
(For Langston Hughes)
In the Moon Time
Girl
Don't You Know
Sweet Willie
Psalm
Nina Simone

Preface

The fiery passion and epigrammatic terseness with which Loretta Burns re-enacts her experiences and observations as an African American woman in contemporary America reveal her as a poet of life who transcends the labels African American, feminist, and/or womanist. Her poetry captures moments and scenes of living that echo her impressions and intuitions of a world trapped between appearance and reality, illusion and disillusion, expectation and realization, the material and the spiritual. Through her deceptive simplicity of diction, she explores the nooks and crannies of her psyche as well as her society's. It is a poetry written from the depths of the heart that calls attention to the mystery and sacredness of the everyday. It therefore comes as no surprise that Loretta Burns and Bill F. Ndi, the Cameroonian-born poet with a fierce drive for global peace and the oneness of humanity, should collaborate on a collection of poems. With vibrancy and a sense of urgency, their lines evoke humanity's perpetual struggle for freedom and its search for meaning.

Part I

Poems by Loretta Burns

La Belle Dame sans Choix

A dark knight
rode a horse
named Jericho

through the narrow streets
of the Quarter
on out beyond the black bayou.

He fell asleep
under a cypress tree
to the screech owl's
mad cry.

He awoke
to pungent grasses,
white oak and Chinaberry,
dogwood and spider lily
deep beds of grape hyacinth.

It was more than pretty.
Jericho drank from a pellucid pool
that shivered
as the wind slid by.

All quiet except
in the distance he thought he heard
a honky-tonk piano.

She came
from a cave

3

In a yellow dress,
with tan hair in coils
and gems on her feet.

She fed him roasted quail,
figs and pomegranate
Brazil nuts and honey,
pumpkin bread and plum wine.

He was nobody's fool,
but when he spied the ruby
on her left middle toe,
he bit his lip to keep from trembling
and dared to speak of love.

She sighed and said,
"A nagging immanence,
a holding off,
lean, desperate.

A far cry."

The knight was full of pain.
He looked around and said,
remembering his Wallace Stevens,
"'And is this all of paradise
that we shall know?'"

She laughed—not in a mean way—
and said, remembering her
John Lee Hooker,
"'Throw your arms around me
Like a circle round the sun.'

The web I am spinning
catches the light."

July South

Here
in Sweet Canaan,
not just the China
berries, red dirt, and
muscadines,
but everywhere
cat bones
and harmonicas.

The dull road winds
to somewhere
around dusk,
when suddenly,
a dogtrot
and gourds painted
lime green.

February Spring

In the morning
I see jonquils jutting
without suspicion.
hear careless cardinals
whistling Dixie,
they are the lucky birds.

I go my way
unbeguiled.
What do they know?
What do they know,
the bird and bush,
of the specter
in the dew drop?

Within the Wheel

Amid the twisted tumult,
sunken faces, flights of armies,
plastic bodies—
the private grief,
a paltry thing,
and yet a little world.
Spiral winds howl
leveling all,
while somewhere in Borneo,
a blond-haired woman shakes,
face down,
wailing trivial tears,
against the wind and rain,
into her grand pillow.

The Man We Killed

The correspondent said
in answer to a question
that things
were going smoothly.
Reported on your candid
yams and TV.
Said your sisters
had come to visit.
Then the anchor
with a cheery OK
broke to the hazardous
waste story.
The victim's mother will
sleep better soon.
A few prayer vigils
here and there,
But you are only a shade—
one minute to midnight,
a shade of a shade.

But I could not close my eyes.

Yet I did sleep
without dreaming
sometime after the end.
And am I any better—
building strophes
out of your bones?
The spirit is wounded.
Arthur Lee, Arthur Lee,

how can I scribble and scratch
these words?
How can I not?

Worm Hole

My world is full
of hummingbirds
and new rising
stars.
Wild honey
tulips and stallions.
The stick lies
on the pillow
rarely used
on a lark
to cast out
dragons.
I know this place
phantasmagorical
full of mayflies
and time.

The Old Scholar

At certain slack hours
when no one knocks,
I can sit quietly here
with the door closed.
I can daydream or doodle,
or wonder what I am doing—
no one will know.
I sit and stare at paintings
or notes to myself on the wall.
The dome and naked trees
outside the window are consoling.
I would rather look out
than crack the door.
One more offering before the day ends,
before the silent ride home.

The Homecoming

The church ladies hugged me
And the men shook my hand.
They saw the child they knew,
had always known,
come back to bathe in their
blessing.
But a sharp-eyes old sister
gave me a quarter
for luck.

After New Orleans

If we've conspired all these years,
even during the silences,
you must know a thing or two
about me.
Some secret place
closed up like a moonflower.

The rain, the heavy air
in the magic city,
crossing the path of some ancient spell,
or going down
under my own thoughts and whispers.

To wink at crystals and desire,
was that her meaning?
What, then, to make of
that old splendor?

Your unsmiling face,
your voice, full of 5's,
reminding me of sweet bread
and early trains.

Is there anything to understand
except in colors of sound?

It's getting late on in the evening,
I feel like going home.

Among the alleyways and live oaks,

surrender to a lovely favor,
a sacred thing,
every day and Sunday,
to come back, to move beyond
the same place.
To crush madly,
with our eyes open,
to breathe
together.

For William

Sometimes
I can see reflected
in your dark eyes
all the old times—
picking roses on our
way to church on Mother's Day,
how you always watched after me
and the time I cried
when you said you were running away.
Miss Simms' piano lessons
and stealing grandmama's apples.
It all comes back
sometimes,
overflowing
like the spirit of prayer.

The Baptizing

They came marching,
the newly saved,
to the water's side.
white-robed witnesses
moaning, "Take me to the water,
to be baptized."
Urged on by the host,
one by one they were
washed in the sacred pool,
and shouted for joy.
An old man feared the water
and wished to turn back
but too late—
the saints would have him.
"Loose him, Satan," they shouted,
"Loose him."
And as they chanted against the sky
he trembled,
fearing
the terrors of hell,
but terrified
of the path to heaven.

Ax Man

The trumpet player walks west
in the nearly dawn,
the echoes of his journey
an indigo haze above
the wounded streets.
He is undone,
still flying
beneath the moon,
still dreaming
the wished for consummation.
His body smokes
as he leans toward home.
A pretty woman waits
to talk of coming rain

Night Song

Suddenly aware
of the silent pines
the murmurs of
invisible archangels
the whistle from
the big mill
Emitt's flute
gently stabbing the dark
you can hear it as well as I
how can you go on eating
that banana
I haven't much fortitude
you know
but I've never set my watch
ten minutes slow
it's not easy
God knows
how to use the toilet
without screaming
that one is lonely in her waiting
can you see her face as well as I
I don't have much fortitude
maybe I will set my watch
ten minutes slow
and flutes make
succulent sounds

Rock Water

Beware
the fatal wedge
of little nothings.
Of words
thrown down,
of silent wounds,
of trifling treachery
unrecorded.

The shroud of memory
outlasts
desire and will.

Love is sea,
Love is sand.

Peaches and Honey

Brilliant eyes bravely

    YOUR MAMA'S IN THE HOSPITAL

Entering this coldness

    YOUR DADDY'S IN JAIL

Where Nature sucks

    YOUR SISTER'S ON THE CORNER

The baby's breath

    CRYIN "LOVE FOR SALE"

Nashville

Edna Mae left her old man
after six years
and took her two babies—Rickie
and Reegie Man—and headed
for Memphis.
Now she's working at
Krispie Chicken and waiting
for a new revelation.

Meeting

pencils, briars,
pigeons, gunboats,
stick people jabbering
like tipsy mice,
vera's husband
has returned
and what to buy
for supper

A Little Blues
(For Langston Hughes)

Another Friday night's done come and gone,
I say another Friday night's done come and gone.
Too late to cry, I just lay in bed and moan.

Sweet papa's gone and I got myself to blame,
Sweet papa's gone and I got myself to blame,
Would call him back, but things wouldn't be the same.

Too tired to work, but I got the rent to pay,
I'm too tired to work, but I got the rent to pay.
I wonder, people, will I always feel this way.

In the Moon Time

In the moon time
listening
to the ticking
of the clock
remembering
a large room
another ticking clock
a weary child afraid of sleep
clutching the strap of your nightgown
the night before you had to leave
"when you get up it's going to wake me
and I can go too"
but when she woke always
you were already gone

Girl

The bride price was six pigs,
twelve net bags,
some axes and arrows.
Your father, smug as a cayman,
talked of planting and fidelity,
coaxed you to sidelong glances
without flinching.
You, thirteen, played with your hands
and scanned the sky
for a *red* bird.

The men came first,
wearing their penis gourds,
pushing the pigs.
The women fanned themselves
before making the bed.
The prize pig
was shot through the heart
and all bore witness.

The dancing and singing
went on all night,
and the wilderness howled
against the crimson moon.

Don't You Know

Ours
is an old story,
full of flame and mist,
notes and rhythms
of miles and trains.
a dream tale at dusk
a quest,
an answer.

The wide river bends,
the moonflowers open,
then the big star falls,
and day is breaking.

The blue of autumn sky
reminds me—
they were right all along,
the lovers.
They were right all along,
but how to tell it?
This cup of grace,
this shimmering thing
we share.

Sweet Willie

It doesn't matter
if you don't
      kiss
      the sun,
it's all in the trying

her paper dolls
      crumpled
and summer ends
but she still sings
in the choir

Psalm

His love surrounds
as my mother's arms,
a velvet cloak
against the chill of night.
His grace, my beacon and high place.
His mercy falls like August rain,
awaited, underserved.
I am His darling,
I cannot leave the light.

Nina Simone

A cauldron of flame,
she sits—majestic, menacing,
a huntress queen.
Rambunctious cry born of eyes
that see too deeply.
Voice in murky fullness
slashes hearts open.

Smoke

I saw the women walking,
walking,
shadows pause,
what ship, where bound?
All night
when I'm sleeping
the women are walking.
For the first time
I saw them,
camellias in their hair,
but they were beyond us,
we beyond them.
Dual planes, one
more real than reality.
I saw the women walking,
such a lonely street.

Mai

What can I call you?
There are no words
warm enough.
I can only liken you
to a mountain spring—
refreshing and eternal—
and from whose depths
I draw my strength

Ebony Angels
(For the black airmen of World War II)

Swing high, Ebony Angels,
swing high, swing high.

You flew farther than you knew.

We stole away with you
from Tuskegee's red clay.
Shielding flying fortresses
in Europe's skies,
outnumbered over Anzio,
the Balkans, North Africa.
And when you stood and waited
we were there.

You, the gallant ones,
strangers in all lands,
seeking, reaching
the sublime.

Gilead

dirt road   barely twilight
dark woman
red head scarf
weary swiftness
walking toward home
a child hurrying
to meet her

Weather Report

train whistle
sound clear this evenin'
rain comin'

So Much for That

The wonder is
that you,
who came so near
the light to me,
stretched out your hands
to let me fall
stretched out your hands
to check me.
I heard the spirits
and I called,
I called your name.
You came
to know me.
And even now,
when things earthbound
would tarnish you,
I know your name,
even now,
I know your name.

Moment in Time

Walking down a hundred
and twenty-fifth,
lost and swirling
in a scarlet space,
suffering the sharp bones
in my back

till an ancient wine man
called to me—
"Hey, girl,
wid yo pretty behind."

Day's End

grey glimpses of buildings
through naked trees,
so soon
winter comes

Street Scene

You got the light lady
but them cars comin' out
from that side street
won't stop.
Light changed again
and you still got to wait.
Wonder if you'll ever
get across,
or will you be trapped
on that corner
forever—
waiting for the right light.

Roland

You remember
the paper church fan
with the boy and girl—
she was the leader—
crossing a broken bridge
over danger waters.
Above, an angel woman hovered,
arms spread, watching.

I dreamt. We two
on a righteous quest.

How excellent
it seemed.
What lavish peril,
what sweet communion,
what blessed assurance.

Part II

Poems by Bill F. Ndi

War Dogs

The dogs' bark never is fun
Who is now dead and gone
With just the mound left behind
Dazzling everybody blind
To any other story that there is
In their lone struggle to settle in peace

Around a pack of rabbit dogs
After them as if hunting hogs
Willing to take blamelessness to the cross
On which innocence is all gain not loss…
For all to wipe their tears
And bury all their fears

In the name of the lamb
Whose light outshines dogs' lamp
Through flesh and blood spilled unjustly
With just hope dogs fall miserably
As the lamb like the tiger strike
And merry make happiness spike.

Poets' Last Words

They may lie dying
With no words drumming
But their blink
Drives to think
Of their endurance
Seeing no one dance
At the time they hope to see
Their love plunge in liberty…
Off they nod without a word
And our loud cries, their last word!

Outside The Purse

When society loses focus
Her poets and scribes must stay focus
As when in marriage
Woman goes in rage
A dutiful husband must she borne
And if let loose, stolen is the fun...!

Focus for cameraman
Focus for the penman
Focus for husbandman
Focus for businessman
Focus for hunter man
Focus for painter man

Focus, Focus, Focus for all man
Focus, Focus, Focus for woman
Keeps world away from loss
And directs the main cause
Our fight would rid of pus
With focus far from purse.

Judge Himself

His robe painted with black blood
His wig whitened with black blood
His crown polished with black blood
His table shined with black blood

His hammer hits black
And black must fight back
For he on black blood cushion rests his back
But self-examining, he won't look back

Hitting the table he shouts out guilty
Forgetting his regalia dyed guilty
On our island of poverty
Making of us poor the guilty

When his forebears were convicts
Just as the poor street addicts
Peddling little antics
Gluing them to street kicks

Tell Mr Judge, "poverty is no crime"
Not even when the poor are his grime
He at least can still intone a chime
That to his peers won't taste like lime

As Lincoln was shocked to see an honest
Man of the trade in his eternal rest
And Mr. Judge needs not do his best
To match the shocking one at rest.

Skin and Heart

Black skin white heart
White skin black heart
All we can change is the skin
Not a heart twisted within.

Shame Game!

Only Van Gogh will handle yellow his way
And none will ever his yellow steal away!
Vagrants brought in something they called development
Leaving and leaving us in total bewilderment
In mid-air hanging
Left today dangling
Between East and West
Knowing just no rest
In their development finely adorned
Hiding within the rotten king they've sworn
To make glitter their yellow
The like of Van Gogh's mellow
And soothing one transporting to haven
As vagrants' snatching it like a raven
Whose beak stuck in its prey paints
 Our earth red with blood of saints
Saints of innocence and weakness
Who pay the price for shamelessness;
Develop strength to crush without shame
For these blameless are a guilty game
In the lord's park
Shy of a lark
To caress his ears
As their cry them sears
So must they their necks to find peace
Noose or at gunshot fall apiece
To stop East West dangling
There and then lasting peace knowing.

A shame game!

A shame game
They've always played;
Progress delayed
Where in their own revolution they glory
Of the weak and innocent they make misery
And pray they remain forever blind
In a world the weak prayed all were kind
Even the man eating kings with big appetite
Who in recent years took pleasure in Apartheid,
A monster, vagrants supported
Condemning all who reported
This shameful gimmick
These gamers mimic!

War Pleasure, Child's Revulsion

When a child spends time scanning the horizon
So does a war monger making his a war zone
With their differences in their hopes
The child sets his hopes atop slopes
Where mongers would drag all down
And have them in the stream drown
As the Sun takes its rise
Some pleasure in their vice
Yet, the child sees not the pleasure
'Coz quest for calm is his nature;
With twilights at dawn or dusk
This child will scent in them musk
Awakening him to his dream adoration
So he can stand and show us his revulsion
For our world to see and follow his wisdom
Taking creeds close to heavenly kingdom
Which must on this earth be lived
Not their hereafter believed
For which the blood thirsty do die
Clueless their cause had been a lie…

Money Slave

Pursue passion! Slave not for money!
Money that would in you spark cruelty
With illusions of strength and might
Unable to change what a mite
From the poor old widow
Did; having the great bow
For such a wealthy heart
Gladly warming like hearths
With worldly paucity
She possessed cheerfully

Sinuous Curves

Snaking way in with a book called good
The book they drop and carry the loot
And in that book we seek the goodness
In our total state of shabbiness
And God will bless Africa
As he's done for Arm licker
Blessing the dollar mightily strong
Weakening us weak for we've done wrong
Showing the plainness of our nakedness
Plain and naked still filled with happiness
Their Godly right on the dollar printed
Which rights poets on earth would not have minted
Poor poets like poor Africa are poor
And their wisdom like that ancient dour
Chides of the folly of human madness
Strike the chord driving insane mundaneness
To purging mankind of constipated book content
Striking and purging work no poet would ever relent
Until they see these international thieves repent
To repent they must humble themselves
And turn upward the forced downward curves.

Dues for Dews

Morning dews like suicidal on leaves hanging
Frightens not but entices to thirst quenching
After a long night of dehydration
Spent in bed that rocks with commotion
Rocking like the sea hidden within dry fish
That would the sea wave have adorned as a dish
But for politicians happy we're hanged like dews
And for which they would we did pay them weighty dues
And the dues we pay hefty and heavy
With no dew drop touching the ground
Near where our footsteps could be found
Yet, morning dew like liberty would always guide;
Guiding us like a groom his way towards a bride
And unlike a groom with fears of what belies in front
Not fear but joys we shall harbour as a unique front
While dressing a brand new bed with liberty
We shall scan liberty and freely too
With evil oppressors have nil to do.

The Longing

I went round looking and looking for little miss pretty
The one I saw close to home went for pa money
So, never was any deal done
For her desire would be foregone
For I had no money but affection
Which in turn stood miles from her attention
And all I could was pray money bought her some
Now that I know pretty is not about form!

Welcome miss hideousness if she has a heart
Not like the gun above pointing at a heart
And with desired money can buy a gun
And same money will never drum the fun:
Affection far from her reflection would
Gently soothe any lost soul in the wood
A dream most will like to have
Than live and die with no laugh.

His Victory

Seeing shark teeth in display drives to thinking
Of smiles brightening His Excellency's win
After promises so untrue and surreal;
Smiling for being propelled to the helm to steal
From the miserable poor, poor miserable misery
Is all the poor plebes are left with as their history
The malapert having his way tricked to the helm
Legates a frightful Jeremiad as an emblem
With brand new egg shells nodding not the doup
Just before they come to see they've been duped.
Behind shark teeth in display is a murder machine
Giving not Rodin's thinker time to support his chin
In pensive moodiness bringing the world to come see
How a sculptor's views dash to and fro across the sea
And His Excellency in this battle won
So, we would acclaim him murderer number one!
When the west his deeds greets those of a strongman
On them we trample as those of a hangman
And sing hangman, hangman!
Your pay is: hang not man!

Tulip Tree Leaves

A tree leaf that says it all
No Bangolanian would fall
Seeing this leaf nor would he stand
And refuse to understand
The call to report back home to ancestors
Who in their graves still grace his life with no gores!
Tulip tree leaf from you I will take no leave
Were the world to care less you were my relief
For those who in you believe the seeds of peace
In them carry the tulip tree leaf of peace
And I bid you! Flourish and flourish!
Even the heart of the Moorish
Desert who rejects the green of your peace
And though its livers do dine on peas

Peace Warring War

All: In the metaphysical properties of the Word we believe!

       In motion, He sets winds of change in this world: a relief!

Poet: What do we want?

Audience: We want Peace!

Poet: What do we want?

Audience: We want Peace!

              We want Peace!

Poet: Where do we differ?

Audience: They want war!

              We want Peace!

              Peace, Peace, Peace,

              We shall drum Peace!

Poet: Peace we shall drum

              Drum, drum and drum

              Peace

Audience: Peeeeeeeeace…!

Poet: Peace we shall drum

              Until for all mankind

              No pains!

              Peace Reigns!

              Creed is for the cretin

              And what's our duty?

Audience: Conscience is our duty!

              And Peace shall Reign

              Come sun come rain,

              And Peace, Peace, Peace

              Shall their war shatter apiece!

Poet: So, What do we want?

Audience:	We want Peace!
Poet:	So, What do we want?
Audience:	We want Peace!
	We want Peace!
Poet:	So, Where do we differ?
Audience:	They want war!
	We want Peace!
	Peace, Peace, Peace,
	We shall drum Peace!
Poet:	And Peace shall Reign
	Come sun come rain,
	And Peace, Peace, Peace
	Shall their war shatter apiece!

Seeds of Peace

You are so tiny
In their world ready
To crush and bury you
With their greed blind to you

Seeds of peace so tiny
The ones I love dearly
To nurture in me the biggest tree
Giving pleasure to the world being free

Under your shade they will sit and stories hear
Of strives and wars nobody will ever fear
For their graves afoot this tree won't your weight bear
And glad we would be with you in us so near

Me, in my grave I'll stroke the root
On which you stand as on good foot
With my remains feeding your leaves
With joy seeing you spread my belief

From birth I bore when all others hope lost
'Coz thin you were and would have entailed cost
Which only patience and faith could come by
Not by their thinking money would you buy

Seed of peace
Tree of peace
Play with the wind the music
That soothes the soul like magic
Fascinating kids and adults

As you had been my catapult
Catapulting the courage and strength
Which in my grave have met me at length

Seeing my dream storybook child love
Flying cherubically above
The buried brutality
They once sang for liberty.

True liberty knows and loves Peace
Not brutalities that them please!
And knowing you all these years, a great bliss
For no good reason I would any dare miss.

Peace Warriors

Vampires shall fly in for a kill
And shall their due have not our will
That has spurn and spurs our undertaking
The one that leaves them shaking and quaking

Vampires welcome for the kill
We shall send you back home ill
When our will has petered your undertaking
Leaving us like tree leaves in sweet breeze, dancing

The Entrails of Thoughts

Philosophy never was wrong
Where human thinking was proved wrong
To thinking thinking needs be in black and white
Whereas black thoughts transferred to us with no blight

Came without ink and sheet
Meeting us in the fleet
With theirs on paper with a pen inscribed
Not ours with the tongue on our minds inscribed

Not with the serpent's hiss
Nor the snaking of the brook its way brooking
Down the valley having us without booking
We would never have missed

Stressing the quintessence of peace
Softening minds like the Golden Fleece
Sweeping away illegitimate rule
Once forced upon our nations as a rule.

Our Leaders & Our drums

They came with veils on their faces
We greeted and drummed their praises!
When the wind brought the stench of their faeces
Our nation stood up to halt the disease;
With her our hammers drummed out! Out! Out!
Yet, to cling, cling, cling they crushed the crowd
With their swords chiming a tune
To bash our hopes out of tune;
Hopes whose strength in non-visibility lies
Will the drum beat them out! Out! Out! With the lies
They had veiled with promises to bring in
And unleash their hounds to bite within
Which they do but our hopes are the last words
To usher them out and bury their swords.

Naming the Culprit

Aids, cholera, malaria…
Plague such countries south of Iberia
With responsibility on bad government
The culprit has always had on as garment
Governments that sit not in laboratories
But to poets' nose stinks like lavatories
As they hear of monstrous profit margin
Announced by banks greeted with sips of gin
By CEOs blooming like water lilies in a marsh
Same as the vulnerable poor litter roadsides like trash
Blown together by promises of an end to their plight
In which mix-up they have been told and told they had
right
Now to name the culprit, unwillingness or bad
government?
Either way the poor lot have to make do with bad
government
Unwillingness to let go some change make the rich stable
With the poor longing for their horses they had a stable
Longing for the culprit? Name names it is a muddle
Stephen Blackpool would never have sought for a
model!

This Duet

Fellow would-be dead poet
Treason sung as a duet
None would want to sing
But this is your thing

For even if you were slain and slain
Your blood will leave indelible stain
On the hands of our blood thirsty guru
Whose evil thinking and cruel deeds do brew

A pot of hemp to deaden the crew's senses
To executing their pointless performances
Having the nation on her knees on a rough surface
And would love us to project this as a smooth surface.

Sing and sing out the hurt
Till guru stops to flirt
And by the horn tackle the bull
And give our nation a kind pull.

Gimmicks King Commander

He only saw himself, chief commander
And how could he get there? Gerrymander
His way to the boxes
Leaving us with losses

He got there!
We are here!
Neither of us blind to that gimmick
Of his rendering the nation sick

Year in year out
He goes not out
Like a canker worm
Eating within form

To leaving the carcass
Of our love no feathers
But wanting us ostrich proud
Thinking us fools in a crowd

But we are a crowd conscious of being fooled
And out of the mess will have ourselves pulled
Even with all his riggings and gun-totting
Hoping we'll yield and yield; that's not our thinking!

Inch by Inch

It was not just the feeling
Inch by inch they came crooking
On their knees

It was not just the sight
Inch by inch they promised no fight
And we went to sleep

Then they started eroding inch by inch
Before we knew they'd signed up for a binge
We'd bidden trouble

So, we signed in for sand bags
They saw in us only rags
They'd shred apiece

In their hopeless design
They dreamt we would resign
We drove them mad

Inch by inch that long awaited feeling
Started creeping in and stimulating
Joys of freedom

Inch by inch their desire
We didn't give them back fire
Leaving them no ash

The storm had come and gone
We have had our job done

Raising the flag of peace

Inch by inch out of the labyrinth
We squeezed the plinth on which stood their myth
And on which pax fly full mast.

One of 5 That Beat 187

Little by little
They spotted dimples
With some before me plodding the beautiful avenues
Those by the Champs-Elysées with so little revenues
Wondering the burning lights in the streets, blind
Where misery plodded hoping for a kind
Mind to embrace
From other race
Without ruffle
Without shuffle
And no thought
Of law or tort
By a palace
With just one place
For a big gun that shoots
Far beyond to kill shoots
In lands so distant
That none a deviant
Would dream but greet a great five
In a council ninety-five
Gets not close to a vote
Where there's no antidote
For bullies had been born
And others can't be sworn
Within the walls impervious to change
Change's not for the castles but the grange
For farmers to till and toil
Not because they own the soil
But are the soils to be shaken off
For these nations to have air enough

In unity they are democratic
For the sixth one just has to boot lick
And if not, all his kind are with sanction
Greeted for they're champions of corruption
Refusing to hold its light
For five to have burden light
'Coz nature designed them on top of this one
To be split apiece as they build block as one
To blacken black, black
When one goes off track
The track of gloom
Set as their boom
Down the spiral
Artificial
Street walls
Like falls
Falling
'n crushing
This black sheep
Bleating sleep
Out of their desire
To forget the fire
They lit to burn black, black
And hail their life with cracks
Revolution can only be white
When 'tis black it is covered with blight
So five must beat one eight seven
What? Five are right to break even…!

Litany of Lamentations

Not just a vicious cycle
I would say a spiral of violence
Not just psychological torture
I would say a nation run by thieves
Not just crushing of youth's dream
I would say killing of the larvae before they grow
Not just a wall made of gangsters
I would say constructed with their bricks of arrogance
Not just haughtily bawdy
I would say morally uncouth
Not just devilishly cunning
I would say satanically sly
Not only the smell of their shit
I would say the stench of rottenness
Not just looking like political mishmash
I would say political indigestion
Not just misery in squalor
I would say abjection in a quagmire
Not just legalisation of corruption
I would say bastardisation of impurities
Not just condoning crime without punishment
I would say consolidation of their heinousness
Not just a throne and crown in decay
I would say their timeless putridity
Not just a king sowing seeds of discord
But I would say but dances and rhy6mes with division
Not just clannishly sheepish
I would say gangsterly arrogant
Not just sloppily clumsy
I would say a thousand headed hydra

Not just monstrously ugly
I would say a basking shark
Not just the flames of passionate hate
I would say unpardonable hellish hate
Not just that they can't change
I would say they've made up their minds impervious
Not just they won't look back
I would say some men can't just change
Not just trapped in their quick sand
I would say misery, poverty and privation
Not just a gang of petty thieves pushed by hunger
I would say highwaymen robbing for greed
Not just a lazy stupid bunch at the helm
I would say a lousy crazy bunch steering the ship
aground
Not just a demagogue thinking he's a pedagogue
I would say a coward with demagogic delirium
Not just fake politicians and statesmen
I would say convoluted to the marrow bone
Not just their disorderly debauchery
I would say chaotic apocalypse now
Not just driving the nation into her grave
I would say making of every life living hell
Not just through blind and questionable greed
I would say through reckless and unthinkable felony
Not just by burning and burning with fire
I would say burning and burning to ash all hopes
When the gangster in chief has to this listen
I would the world ask him what he has learnt as a lesson.

Really Odd

Murderer, murderer kill your corruption!
And from us receive an ovation.
Sad sights on our streets with slain liberty
Your garb colours full bright ignominy
When on innocence your wickedness you unleash
And would the world enjoy it their favourite dish

Murderer, murderer why not kill all wars
To have thanks from us all fill your purse?
With this plague everywhere in our world
Our hopes for lasting peace on fears board
'Coz you can't withstand your thirst for blood
One we come to grade as really odd!

Murderer, murderer your acts kill true needs
For even madmen chastise your deeds
Insane enough for them to reason
And take a distance from their season
Of madness to have us dance with them
The tune of life plagued with a problem.

Feeding the Baobab Tree

Though fresh it looked
Anger it hooked!
From whence it's seed
Given no heed
For being tiny
Chose trendy
saw
across

                                         this ready

           remedy

                applause !
that baobab tree
sat in our yard
many centuries
yes it grew fat
and we grew thin
and it came to pass
it swallowed in
not our bright stars
our lamentations
fed it this fat
not confrontations
nor aims with darts
yet, it brought us together
to sit, stories tell and hear
know
no
saw!

To slit our throat
For shame's clean coat
By our leaders worn
For which they're not sworn.

Flower Pot Music

Would   no   one   tell   the
     world
Of   melodious   mused   word
Adorning   my   computer
Singing so sweet potted flower
Music no   one   hears
Even those with ears
But the eyes on which she strikes the chords
Softly and carefully against odds
The pot the drum
Does the heart plumb
The flower
The drummer
Sending one up the ladder of joy
And up he should go without being coy
Ready to feast the eyes
Like a child sighting rice
Without price weighing on his kind
In a world none has him in mind
Safe flower pot drumming colour
Spurring tears of joy not dolour
Saying why no one hears
'Coz the lot harbours fears.

We Shan't Perch

kill   peace slyly
her music has just
far from dust
been really
soft so
and called for no
knell, bell, snell, cell, gel,
smell, yell, spell, girl, fell…
shot hunting change for all
but stood tall,
treating waste matter
she is a master
no mistress
would with mess
So she won't look
nor utter a yelp at the fluke
blinking bs
on whom should be unlocked swarms of bees
to buzz change with e in their ears
and hoping one of their ears hears
not the soft music
but the pain with which all is sick
of them dreaming in silence we die
round the clock we shall tell them they lie
for we are birds from hunters fleeing
if power-tricksters think themselves hunters shooting
without missing
we shan't perch
as we for peace search.

Peaceful Lake of Peace

This peaceful lake of peace is in Ndop
There, the rice field green better soothes mankind
In which lake, for a swim war can't drop
As Christians, Muslims and animists bind
Their strength in being to each other
Kind and would go a step further
They would go this step to embrace
Embrace each other not their craze
Driving our world to the extremes
We woke up to find were not dreams
Crashing on towers high as Babel
And ringing of madness its warning bell
Greeted by the West with madness
Which does steal away happiness
With just thought of lake burning its flames
So sane should avoid shifting blames.

On The Stage

Seeing with the naivety of a child
With the raucous laugh of an imbecile
Expressing with the wisdom of a sage
And like a scavenger digging knowledge
Living in this world with the sight of a blind
Who to see, only does with one thing, the mind
Yelling out like a child parents can't stop
Yelling till he sees the king quake and drop
Finding in you
These Kings will spew…
No, puke! Puke out their guts
Seeing you poets with guts!

True Mother

In the morning a cock crows
A true mother hearing knows
As would cry from her child
When from the heart a child
Does cry
Such cry
A heart pained by Delilah's daughter
Solace does come quick eased by mother
With her words the tears sponging,
Healing broken heart's longing.

Now the heart does know
Who'd the towel throw?

Eve's daughters are not all Delilahs
Not even when their acts echo hers…!

Our Big Heads

Big heads multiply their blunder
Canonising striking plunder
Sapping from the taproot of nations
To leaving nations desperations
Cutting a quarter moon smile on their faces
Forgetting this is just one of the phases
The moon comes up with to blind the night
And spin their heads to see the wrong light
And discard the masses as scums of the earth
Deserving of nothing terrestrial but dearth
Which children in dream tear to pieces
Like the tiger its prey as it pleases
Just the like of heads delighting in the game
Blundering in our streets, looting with no shame
Defining that trade
In favour of eight
Unfolding their blood stained carpet of negligence
On which they display claims of divine providence

Peace Warriors

Vampires shall fly in for a kill
And shall their due have not our will
That has spurn and spurs our undertaking
The one that leaves them shaking and quaking

Vampires welcome for the kill
We shall send you back home ill
When our will has petered your undertaking
Leaving us like tree leaves in sweet breeze, dancing

Love Sake

Hit your chest and look at me as a fool
'Coz on me everyone sits as on a stool
Yet, I thought I'd be your throne
Not knowing you'd have me thrown
But as a fallen man I fear no fall
And laugh at sacks of flesh and bones up tall
In pride and arrogance
Only to fall in trance
Moved by the spirit that humbles
So that no soul ever crumbles;
The spirit in the fallen man
Would never leave any man wan!
Instead of hitting your chest
Priding in what's in your chest,
Hug and embrace a poor fool
Whose spirit makes a good stool
On which wise men will sit
For your kind to smell shit
And leave them in a bind
Simply for they're love blind,
Blind for that's the nature of love
And the love buck's always told off.